My Embrace

Inspiring stories, thoughts and poems
about living with fear, compassion, humor and love.

Lori Joseph

for:
Jasmine,
Many Hugs & Much Love
Lori J.

Cover Design and Illustrations by

Rich Mills, Streamrun Studios, LLC

My Embrace

ISBN-13: 979-8-642-23815-8

For Carter

Contents

Introduction

Several years ago, I became completely captivated with the magic of words as I began writing poetry. As I write, I become a conduit for the water droplet, the blade of grass, the little girl, the farmer, all wanting to share their story. Often transporting me to an unfamiliar world yet feeling so natural. The first time I circulated my poetry manuscript to friends, their immediate response was, "You're brave." Honestly, bravery never crossed my mind. I simply became a messenger delivering the news.

Sharing this collection of thoughts and stories with you feels right. I hope my reflections inspire you to take the ordinary and become extraordinary.

*Just the other day I sat in complete wonderment.
Have you ever given thought to how many people have
served you in your lifetime, or simply in your daily life?
Think of the farmers, truck drivers, technicians, military
personnel, law enforcement officers, artists, musicians,
pilots, postal carriers, mechanics, restaurant staff,
plumbers, caregivers, and on and on . . .
Wowza! How did we get so lucky?*

Feeling grateful for all the Doers in the world and You!

From the Fire

Did you ever have something catch you completely off guard but you knew you had to act on it? On an early summer afternoon, I stepped outside of the photography studio in Fort Collins, Colorado, to begin my drive back to Nebraska. The sky was the color of burnt sienna, the air thick with smoke. Over the course of a week, 87,000 acres in the mountains west of Fort Collins burned along with 259 homes and one life, Linda Steadman. While in the area, I learned of the fire's impact and how the locals had been working diligently, offering food, blankets, and trailers to move livestock, and volunteering in whatever way they could to help their community. I traveled home with their situation in my rearview mirror and in my heart.

The following morning, I went for a walk and considered how those affected by fires must feel. I wanted them to know they weren't alone and that people throughout our country genuinely cared for them. My idea was to have artists create lasting pieces of artwork using wildfire charcoal and then sell the artwork to raise money for the Poudre Canyon Fire Department. With that intention and the help of Colorado native Tim O'Hara, the Ashes to Art Project 2012 (A2A) was created. With permission from the Bureau of Land Management, we went to the mountain and collected fragments of charcoal. On our knees, amidst the charred forest, we had hope. I took the bins of charcoal home and began searching online for willing artists in every state. With a map of the USA and push pins, I kept track of my progress.

The timing of this project was tricky since it was just prior to the presidential election. Our concern was that we would lose public interest the closer we got to the election; therefore, artists were given only six weeks to complete the artwork and ship it to Tim O'Hara's photography studio.

Several days before the artwork was due, Tim secured a TV interview with Denver's Channel 9 News reporter Gary Shapiro. Do you have any idea what it's like to do a TV interview? Live? I was shaking in my boots with self-doubt. At the time of the interview, we had only received three pieces of the anticipated artwork! There I was, on television, counting on the promise of others to make the Ashes to Art Project 2012 become a reality.

Three days prior to the deadline, artwork began rolling in, bringing a flood of emotion with each piece we opened. We invited the Poudre Canyon Fire Department to come to the studio to see what their neighbors across the country had created on their behalf. The artwork was impressive, but with the firefighters came reverence. Listening to their testimonials about having been on the front line of the fire was humbling.

Next, Tim O'Hara photographed the artwork for the online auction. Another facet I had never done before. I worked with Bidding For Good, a nonprofit auction site, to guide me through the process. In addition to using

Facebook, I designed cards for the artists to send to their supporters to help spread the word. Tim's connections in Colorado led to interviews with several newspapers and a radio spot to promote our campaign.

In a short time, we led a national campaign that garnered fifty-eight artists from twenty-seven states to create artwork using the collected wildfire charcoal. Artists not only created but also shared profound personal stories of healing and rebirth. We were wholeheartedly touched by their generosity and willingness to share our vision. I am happy to say all of the artwork sold in the online auction with the proceeds going directly to the fire department.

My hope in sharing this story is that you will be encouraged to listen to that voice within, like I did. Until I took that walk, I never imagined leading a national campaign. I didn't know how to do it or if I could even get anyone to believe in this mission as much as I did. But empathy prevailed and I knew I had to listen to the voice inside me and take a chance no matter what.

Through the benevolence of Jim Felix of The Supply Cache, Tim Joseph, my talented book designer, and Tom Turner, our friend and print broker, we provided participants with a beautiful hardback book of the entire collection, which included drawings, paintings, sculptures, glass, jewelry, and a 3D wall hanging. Extra books were sold with proceeds also benefiting the fire department.

Here are a few excerpts from the Ashes to Art book:

The destruction and aftermath of this one fire surpassed the combined effects of all the fires I witnessed in the previous twenty-five years. Some of the greatest losses were by the very same people who spent weeks helping to put out the fire.

Jim Felix, Owner/CEO,
The Supply Cache

But out of the charred remains came a spirit of cooperation that no fire could ever snuff out.

Stacy Nick, *Coloradoan* Arts and
Entertainment Reporter

From the burned out forest of Colorado,
you sent me the charcoal
four distinct chunks, porous, black and cracked
like layers of the earth's strata,
the story of its life now in my hands,
smudged with remembrance.

I will let these majestic trees speak,
even from their ashen body
of what heat and fury, what roar and sounding
as animals fled, humans gathered
and winged ones took flight.

And when I cook my food slowly
like I do every season, the wood
from the forest my fuel
I say a prayer, to the glory of trees and life
to the brave people who donned their suits
and honor and headed into the chaos of fire
to the ones who didn't make it
and the ones who did, the new green
will bloom again.

Heidi Daub,
Maine Artist

A few months had gone by when I was contacted by a staff member from the University of Northern Colorado, asking if I would participate in a workshop for teachers, titled Mapping New Terrain: Arts Applied, to share my Ashes to Art Project experience. I said Yes! I was both thrilled and horrified.

When I hung up the phone, the conversation that went on in my head was something like this:

> *You don't have a bachelor's degree. What could you possibly teach the educated? You've never taught a workshop. What is the most important take-away message you'd like them to hear? Are educated adults willing to hear that they should trust their gut and feel motivated to take the steps when opportunity presents itself?*

As I paced the room and toyed with my approach to leading a workshop, my eyes fell upon a very large stuffed black bear sitting in the corner. Immediately, I went to the computer and discovered the mascot for the university is none other than a bear. According to Native Americans, the bear represents courage, strength, and wisdom. This was a sign. A sign for me to move forward with the workshop and keep it playful.

To engage participants, I took the bear to the workshop and explained how the bear represents opportunity when we rely on our own courage, our own strength, and wisdom.

I opened with how the scent of a campfire can lead us to recall memories of sitting around the fire. The taste of food cooked on an open fire, the crackling of burning wood, the look of the flames, and the feel of the heat all awaken our senses.

With that mindset, I shared how a lightning strike became a wildfire, creating an entirely different tone. I let them consider the destruction and the displacement of people and animals from their homes. We talked about the painful rawness exhibited by firefighters, residents, and the artists and considered our own vulnerabilities.

After review of the artists' bios and artwork, and with the use of props, each participant was challenged to assume the identity of one of the artists. We talked about how the project personally affected them (the artists) and how those feelings impacted their creations. Next, in response to their own emotions, the class was tasked with creating with charcoal from the wildfire.

Some teachers felt vulnerable acting and drawing in front of their peers while others readily performed. Some opened up, sharing how they've let fear keep them from taking chances in life. I closed the workshop noting that everyday experiences can provide us with opportunities when we listen to our intuition.

Had I let my vulnerability and fear hold me back, I wouldn't have created the A2A Project. I knew in my heart I had to try. Even when we don't know all of the hows, whys, and what-ifs, when we rely on faith, we are given the resources and the ability to try. Did I experience moments of doubt? You betcha. And you know, it was at those moments I would receive a call or a note to keep going. I feel confident in telling you to go on and reach when you get the nudge to do something from the heart. You won't be disappointed.

A note from Connie Stewart, PhD, Executive Director of the University of Northern Colorado.

Lori,

Your kind and generous contributions to the CIAE Institute made it one of the best! Somehow you were able to make every one you met feel like they had been your best friend forever! And you were the one who could demonstrate how art responds to current "issues" or events. I do hope we can work together again. Please keep in touch.

Connie

The workshop was evaluated by participants and received a 5/5 status.

The Ashes to Art Project 2012 was included in the History of Colorado Museum exhibit for the Colorado Wildfires.

You Made It!

Like a baseball player sliding into home plate.
Now brush yourself off and give yourself a pat on the back.

Location, Location, Location. We know it's important, but did you know it can be miraculous? The next couple of stories are from a time when I lived on a wooded mountaintop overlooking the Nippenose Valley.

The property had perennial gardens, grape vines, fruit trees, a small barn, and a pool. Backed by hardwoods, layers of rhododendrons, azaleas, magnolia trees, and lilac bushes created a picturesque setting. The first time I stepped foot on the property, I went directly to a path that took me farther into the woods. I felt something stir in me. I didn't have to go into the house to know that it was the perfect place for our family. I often marveled at the morning light that passed through our front door, illuminating our entry. This house was enchanting, as every window offered beautiful views of the natural elements surrounding us.

A church with a steeple that reached to the clouds anchored the community. Adjacent to it was a cemetery, and across the street was a convent. We passed these sights every day while going to and from our new home. One day I saw an Elmo balloon floating above the gravestones. My heart led me to stop and pay my respects to some little soul that had been taken too early in life. I didn't know Molly, but the tears I shed for her and her family were beyond what I had anticipated.

Several days later, I attended a high school basketball game where I met Karen, a parent of one of the players on my son's team. We sat and visited, and she asked where we were living. I told her we bought a house, just past the church on Jacks Hollow Road, and for some unknown reason, while watching our boys run the court, I felt compelled to tell her of my experience at the cemetery. Karen's eyes suddenly filled with tears, causing mine to do the same. She told me she had placed that balloon on her granddaughter's grave. I asked if she had a photograph of her granddaughter to share with me. As if a light switch was flipped on, Karen smiled and grabbed her wallet to show me Molly's picture. She told me no one had ever asked to see her granddaughter and thanked me for caring enough to stop at the cemetery.

Patience, Come!

Because we lived in the woods, we routinely let our dog out to take a run and do his business. In turn, I regularly went out onto our deck calling for Patience, our dog, to come back. Day after day, I'd call, "Patience, come!"

I can only imagine what the nuns must have thought of the poor woman in the woods with four sons calling for "Patience" every day! With any luck, they were praying for our family.

The Prayer

Spring arrived and I found myself spending countless hours at the Little League complex and becoming friends with the families attending the games. William and Mary often came as they had a number of grandchildren playing. That year, William was stricken with cancer, and he lost his battle shortly after baseball season ended. His wife, Mary, reminded me of so many women her age who had worked tremendously hard raising a family, attending church, and loving their family. With her positive outlook on life, conversations with Mary were easy.

About six weeks after William's death, I felt the pressure of someone's thumb on my shoulder. No one was in the room with me. A voice in my head said, "Buy Mary a rose." I was in the middle of life, working, with sons dashing in all directions. I pushed the notion aside, but it became persistent. Every morning I would get this message and feel a pressure on my shoulder! I continued to push it aside. Several days went by and this feeling of pressure was now in the car with me as I drove to town. I was unsure what to do with this thought, this feeling, until it came on even stronger. I turned my car around and drove directly to the florist.

The logical part of me asked, "What on earth would Mary think of me if I appeared on her doorstep with a rose?" We were friends but I didn't know her that well.

I thought maybe a poinsettia wouldn't look so odd, since it was Christmastime. As I considered the different flowers, I knew in my heart it had to be a rose. When I arrived at her house, I was trembling. Unsure of what to say or why I was chosen to deliver it to her, I had to roll with it. She answered the door and was surprised to see me standing there with a rose. When I told her what had been happening to me, she fell into a sob. Once she regained composure, Mary told me she had been praying to St. Therese to send her a rose, signifying her prayers were answered and William was at peace. You just never know who will show up in your life and for what purpose.

Whatever you do today, big or small, you will catapult someone's life when your action comes from the heart.

Thanks for being Amazing!

Taking inventory can be a tedious exercise
but also a rewarding one.
Today's a good day to list all of your accomplishments,
big and small.
You took baby steps, then ran and leaped,
and oh yes, you took flight!

Grateful for movement in our lives.

People go to the gym to improve.

They do strength training, core training,
reps, and cardio conditioning.
Today would be a good day to improve
your mind and your heart.

Ready Set Go

For every doubt you have, think of three
accomplishments you've made.
For every time you get up from your desk or
leave your car, take a nice deep breath.
For every negative person you encounter—
are you ready for this?—reach out and
give them a big virtual hug and
mindfully see them in a better place.

Not only are you improving, but you are
making a difference in the world.

Reflection

When I look in the mirror, I am searching for answers.
I draw close and look into the eyes of the woman
looking back at me.
Who is she?
There are days when I feel simply radiant
and enjoy the reflection.
Then there are the times when I don't
recognize her at all.
How is it I can be looking in the same mirror,
in the same room, at the same face,
and yet come away with such different interpretations?
I don't do this exercise for vanity;
I do it to try to find myself.

I think of the lines, those of character of course,
how they lend themselves to outlining my journey,
highlighting laughter and accentuating times of trial.
I believe my eyes to be my best feature.
They are hazel with lots of amber.
My full lips have retained their rosy contrast
to my complexion.
My life's road map is in the mirror.
By changing my thoughts, I witness immediate change.
I can control how I act and respond,
What I choose and don't,
Love of life, projects.

I know when I feel happy, strong and confident,
I will attract the same,
This contagious energy, this love of self.

Recognizing this transformation
reminds me to be grateful.
The practice of taking a moment to reflect,
To look beyond the skin, to enter the soul,
Find contentment, wisdom and desire.
Take a good look, journey within.
Tell me what you see.

Always remember you are enough.
Now take all of you and radiate that confidence.

In case you didn't know, it's very fetching.

Do you ever wonder how your tag reads?
You know how flooring, kitchen equipment, and
furnishings have a commercial grade option?
I bet "really living life, doing for others, showing up, and
repeating, Commercial Grade" would be on your tag.
Way to Go!

Now what would you name your company?

Feeling grateful for daydreams.

Rediscover Your Innate Ability

We are capable of healing a lot of things in our body without the use of pharmaceutical drugs. Holistic care is on the rise and has greatly increased in the past decade. Over the years, I have explored the use of reiki, spiritual healers, meditation, sound therapy, feng shui, myofascial release, acupuncture, massage, reflexology, kinesiology, aromatherapy, and essential oils. When we are open, willing to try alternative medicine, transformation happens within our body.

Do you remember Unilever's three-minute self-perception study for women, using a forensic artist? The ad became the most-watched internet commercial of all time with over 114 million views in more than 110 countries. The study revealed that women doubt their beauty. I will further say we doubt our ability, way too much.

I hope I live to see the day when insurance companies will cover holistic treatments for Well Being. In fact, it will be fantastic if Dr. Mark Hyman and his colleagues' findings come to fruition sooner than later. They are projecting current illnesses and diseases will no longer exist when the majority of people conceive how our microbiome, our gut bacteria, regulate and communicate with all parts of our body. Now think about that. When our food source creates an imbalance in our gut, every function in our body suffers, including our intuitive ability.

The more we empower people to develop their innate ability to heal, the more likely we'll see them exhibit greater self-confidence. Have fun exploring alternative options for Well Being.

Strut Your Stuff

Make it Happen

Why?

BECAUSE YOU CAN!

It Is In Me

The essence of being,
the familiarity to our senses
takes us on a journey to a day once before
when time was never measured.

To play at water's edge,
where waves tumble and sandcastles are built.
The smell of salt air and the call of shorebirds.
Barefoot in the sand
the tide's power submerges me into nature.

A walk in the forest,
heightened by the fragrance of wildflowers,
shafts of sunlight illuminate the fern beds.
Touching textured bark and feeling moss,
the taste of teaberry and mint.

Visiting the farm,
feeding the calves from a bottle.
Freedom when jumping from the loft into the hay below.
Saturated with the scent of livestock and grain,
tractor and wagon rides over the countryside.

Learning to garden,
on my knees with my hands in the richness of the soil.
Planting with anticipation of what will flourish.

Vegetables eaten fresh and raw,
flowers cut to adorn the table.

Kayaking lakes and rivers,
the feeling of buoyancy and independence.
Turtles and fish rising on the water's surface.
Enveloped in the thermal of this new horizon,
shimmering reflections of birds and clouds overhead.

Skiing the mountains,
crisp clear days with a stark contrast of white against the
cerulean skies.
Trails outlined with sparkling ice-laden trees.
Quietness of skis descending the slope,
fresh air fills my lungs, fills me.

I can travel there any time I choose, for it is in me.

Imagine you are fifteen years old today.
What would you tell your older self?
Call your friends, pick up concert tickets,
eat a slice of pizza late at night, ride your bike?

At fifteen, we no longer had recess but could still play.
Today is a good day to think of ways to PLAY ... and PLAY!

Feeling grateful for Imagination!

When we sit in a gentle breeze and feel it envelop us,
it comes to remind us of all the possibilities.

Smile and know you are a part of
this magical process of life.

Confidence can be so attractive.
Go ahead. Relax, saunter a bit. It keeps people guessing.

Feeling grateful for fabulous shoemakers!

The Meadowlark Sings

It's ninety-four outside
and still as an empty rocking chair.
Mother insisted on visiting the vacant homestead
to retrieve a memory or two.

I stamped down the weeds bursting with grasshoppers
to clear a path for her.
Holding my arm to steady herself,
she told me the boards above the porch,
the ones splayed like piano keys,
reminded her of the music, the dance and the laughter
that once shook the horsehair and lath.
On Saturday nights they'd open the door
and roll up the rugs to create a dance floor,
welcoming folks to celebrate life.

We stood for a reflective moment,
I felt her pat my hand,
she had relived enough and was ready to go.

The following evening and for many to come
I revisited the old homestead
where the door's still open
and the meadowlark sings.

*You can pick and choose and celebrate
all the little touches you do to make others feel good.
Pretty spectacular if you ask me.*

Grateful to make choices.

Grandmother's Garden

I listen to piano music and play on the keyboard
of my writing
I hear songbirds and a slow melody that is constant
It takes me past the picket fence,
into the garden at the rear of the cottage
There is an empty hammock, a fire pit
A child's swing hanging from the live oak tree
The gentle breeze causes the poppies to sway
The swing to move ever so slightly
The lull of the stream makes its way up the bank
Through the fragrant perennial gardens
I sit in the faded chair that my grandmother once used
Wondering about the thoughts she had
in her private oasis
Pondering her children's future as she pulled the weeds
Days when she would take her troubles to the garden
to amend the soil
Earth moist and cool under her feet covered
with fresh grass clippings
Dew glistening like diamonds, resting on Lady's Mantle
Sweet memories
Reminiscing about Mother's Day
when her sons planted the lilac tree in her honor
Peonies, azaleas, dogwoods, rhododendrons
and laurels offered her seasonal retreat
When money could not afford her the luxury of travel

She journeyed quite far in her backyard
with family and friends
Stories of travels to Africa and Rome,
oceans fished and plays performed
Tents sheltered the princess and warriors
Illuminated in the moonlight,
this refuge becomes ever more enchanting
Dancing fireflies and candlelight
accentuate the magic of this garden
She lovingly embraced

Early this morning, I worked in my flower gardens,
weeding, pruning, and planting.
This technique can be used every day.
Live with intention by weeding, pruning, and planting.

It's exciting to nurture your vision.

Grateful for gardeners.

Nostalgia serves us well—
While warming our hearts, we get to see our past journey.

What will you do today to evoke
those feelings years from now?

Think of the times when you've been completely
amazed at the unexpected
and how things worked out in your favor.
Today is a good day to imagine more Favors,
meant especially for you.

I thought that would bring a smile to your face.

Listen, what speaks to your soul today?
Do colorful balloons or the scent of
fresh baked goods make you smile?

Make a simple thought-adjustment. Sway your mood.

Concerto Amour

The sound of the oboe pulls at my fingertips,
coaxing me to step into your world.
Filled with wonder, I do.

I see the back of a pianist poised and rocking as he plays.
People are mingling, spirits are high.
Sparkling sunlight pours
through floor-to-ceiling windows.
Chandeliers and champagne become prisms,
Filling the air with dancing stars and sequins, I dream . . .
You, across the room, laughing, engaged,
Familiar slope of wide shoulders,
Rough beauty I touched, I remember.
Will you turn to me?
I wonder, pearls press the pulse of my throat
and you turn.
Music becomes background and the dancers,
No longer bright enough to hold court,
Scatter politely to frame our reflection,
this fragile slip in time.
It's as if they know, awaiting love's reunion.
I focus on your hands, the very ones that placed
these pearls around my neck with a tender parting kiss.
I dare not meet your eyes, at least not here, not now.
I lay my hand atop the piano feeling the melody's vibration.
I am consumed with memories, of escapades or dreams.

I shall not want to know the truth.
We know this old song, I say;
your hand covers mine in response.
Take me in your dream, I say;
the room tilts and sways in response.
This was never a dream, you whisper;
light turns to night in response.

The oboe fades too soon,
I strain to hear the last note dissolve,
Then turn to grieve in my pillow.
If I had looked into your eyes, where would we be?
Here now, I'm drawn from bed to window,
rest my head to the glass.
Night flight through the formless forever, listening.
The party carries on.
There are dances and then there are dances.
There are lifetimes and then there is you.

Co-written by Judy Burch and Lori Joseph

Marriage

He said, "I thought you wanted my honest opinion?"
She said, "I thought I did too!"

Pushing through the uncomfortable is key.

Standing water becomes stagnant.
With water accounting for over half our body weight,
it's necessary to move.
The earth spins, the sun and the moon rotate, tides flow,
and yes, you are a part of this energy force.

Grateful for radio waves and ocean waves.

Catch and Release

The principle of catching and letting go
Traveling to far off places the fisherman fuels his soul
Yearning to make the catch of a lifetime

Engaging stream entomology
Skillful casts are rewarded with a mere nibble
Studying the riffles, the bend, lush embankments

Last night's stars dance on the water's surface
Reminding him of her eyes
Where they sat next to the fire the night before

Stepping deeper into the current
Enveloped in wilderness
His primal connection was resurrected
With a barbless hook

Candor of the Heart

When a heart suspects,
the rose will drop paranoid petals across the floor
for only you to see
before closing the door.

Carousel

My heart knows of you and me
Yesterday's thoughts relevant
In your eyes
As a flower reaches for light
I want for you
No matter darkness or day
I drift up and down
Waiting for my chosen
On the merry-go-round
Eagerly, anxiously awaiting
Love to circle
Thrill of arrival
Torment of departure
All becomes a blur
Spinning dreams
A reckless act
Painted harness
I cannot hold

Texts, emails and tweets are sent quickly,
often without much thought.
Searching for the right words can sometimes delay
communication but could be worth the wait.

Maybe it's time for you to send someone
you love a handwritten letter.

Grateful for the pen and paper to slow us down.

Like items in a pocket,
you may sometimes feel lost or forgotten.

Reflect on the moment you discovered something
valuable in your pocket—missing keys, the baby's
pacifier, or maybe even some money. That very
instant of discovery contains surprise and gratification.
Now hold onto that feeling. You are valued.

Oh, and it looks so good on you!

Grateful for reflective moments.

No matter how good things roll along, life
inevitably throws in a challenge to help us grow.
Our personal reaction to those hurdles is what
we need to focus on. Are you responding with
compassion and love or anger and hurt?
Only you have the ability to look inward
to create peace in your heart.

"I love you, Little Fishy," spoken by Carter, age two,
as he released a minnow back into the lake. Like Carter,
send Love into the world today. It makes you stronger
for when those challenges show up.

Enduring a Tough Life Lesson

I met a woman when I moved to New England. She was raised on the Gold Coast with a butler and nanny, yachts, and such. We found it convenient to grab a cup of coffee and take walks together, as she was my next-door neighbor and close in age. This convenience came at a price. As I shared some of my personal background of photography styling and catering, she responded by letting me know she had done all of that years ago. In fact, she had even been a model. I found the tone of her response to be discrediting and somewhat hurtful.

As I weighed our compatibility, I decided I needed to continue to be open-minded and learn from this acquaintance, and that I did. The more we walked, the more she talked. As it turned out, she hired caterers and stylists but didn't actually do the work herself. Our walks were always scheduled around her AA meetings, which had been going on for decades. Because I have friends and family who struggle with addiction, I extended my support and understanding.

One day she announced she was having a special celebration. The invitations were professionally printed, and she planned to have "silver service" for this black-tie event. She asked to borrow some of my table decorations, and as a helpful soul I offered to create her centerpiece. She later remarked that she had been delighted to take credit for the beautiful table since I wasn't invited to the party. I later learned she borrowed the silver service too. I seriously don't think she was remotely aware of how her actions affected me. In all honesty, I'm not sure why I felt like a child not measuring up!

What I learned from this encounter:

I had to forgive myself for allowing someone's privileged background to make me feel less or unworthy. Letting go of my insecurities allowed me to regain compassion for her and see our differences more objectively. We all have baggage that needs to be checked at the door. This experience has enabled me to grow.

No Thank You

*My empathy is given with love but
your actions suggest abuse.*

I don't allow people to abuse me.

If you are struggling with finding a solution to something, why not have a little fun and explore something completely unrelated? Stepping away from our problems and finding joy in something else elevates our energy, attracting more that is good.

A recent tour of Mount Vernon revealed that a filmmaker was completely surprised when he drew his inspiration from visiting the ice house.

Grateful to explore.

Do you know the times when you feel
like the deck is stacked against you?

It's likely to bring your vibration down
if you remain there in thought.

Here's a new way to look at it:

Maybe you weren't supposed to be there in the first place.

Pick a new game to play.

It's all about choice.

Despicable

Being a victim of wire fraud, six-figure wire fraud, shook me to my core. The fact that there are people in this world who make a living robbing others is despicable. I write to shed its impact. I write to inform my readers that they, too, can work to overcome life's hardships.

The closing on the sale of our house was the last appointment on a Friday afternoon. When the funds didn't go into our bank account on Monday morning, I discovered our closing had been hacked. Desperate, I ran into the closing agent's office. I didn't go in screaming, but I did go in expecting miracles. Confidently, I told the agent, "We have a problem, and I know we can stop the thieves." The agent later told me it was because of my conviction that she acted so quickly on my behalf to try to get the wire transfer stopped. To assume it would be resolved quickly was completely naive on my part. I went through the gamut of emotional distress. Vulnerability was a big part, but let's add rage, humiliation, and lack of trust. Let's add failure, inadequacy, unworthiness. Let's add compassion, strength, and faith. Yes, you read that correctly. Although it was a huge financial hit, we still had our health, our family, and our friends. This is where my faith had to play a bigger role than the acts of such criminals.

With each day, I knew how important it was for me to try to hold onto a positive mental attitude. To focus on our blessings. The thieves broke our bank account, but they weren't going to break me. Eventually, we recovered a portion of the money but it took years.

On a scale of 1 to 10 (10 being the highest), **where is your Positive Mental Attitude?**

Do you need a reset? If so, try this technique: Imagine placing your challenges, hurt feelings, or anything causing discomfort into a small box and closing the box. This visualization creates separation between you and the issues, enabling perspective. Be kind to yourself.

Resolution

On the surface, everything is all right.
Within, everything should be all right.
In time, everything will be.

Take a deep breath and saddle up for the ride.

Cowboys get weary too.

Challenges offer us the opportunity to discover solutions.

Never to worry. But of course, you already knew that.

*Go on about your day and give someone
a smile they're not expecting.*

Grateful for dentists and mechanics.

Watching dolphins and sincerely hoping to move through my day as gracefully as they do.

Pulse

*Can you imagine what it would sound like to silence
everything except heartbeats and have them amplified?*

Think about metals, their integrity, usefulness,
reflective properties, and finish.
The earth provides the "ore."
Your body has a "core."
Envision all you have accomplished
with your integrity and usefulness.
Pretty darn good, right?

Shine on.

Another Day for Trains

The trains awake me in my slumber
The rumble of their weight on the tracks courses thru me
I toss and turn to find my direction
The whistle blows in the cold stillness
Calling me to find my path
I am here but for a moment
Realizing my life's crossroad
Conductor signals louder and more incessantly
I've grown to learn their sounding is as individual as we
all are on this earth
Some play their horns as if there is no tomorrow
Others merely toot to remind me of their passing thru
Just like the souls
Electing to go thru life, passing onto the next
Sometimes I lie awake and await their arrival
Anticipating who is out there and why they are calling
There are times when the trains cross paths
East meets West
The energy on this planet
The constant motion
I stir
To find my feet and body across the bed
Directions have changed course
There comes a silence and I arise
Walking the dark hallway into the gently
illuminated landing of the stairs

Lighting a candle to sit and meditate
Asking for guidance
Praying for those around me
Yearning to find my way
Why am I here
What purpose do I have here on earth
The trains are gone for this moment
Feeling relief
I often find them maddening
Do I need to be a better listener
Can I truly help to heal those in need
Derailment is only temporary
Each day the trains reappear
With the promise of try again
Their sturdiness weathers the elements
Some are empty and travel hollow
The heaviness of full cars sounds their weight
The cars have attracted some to write their graffiti
The testament of self-expression for the world to see
Is it a cry for help or just a flag to say hey I'm out here

For when they write the train is motionless
They can't even feel the rumble under their feet
Only the cold steel beneath their hands
What goes thru their mind
Did they lose their way

East meets West today
Lifting them in my thoughts
Surrounding them in love and light
I hear the next train coming
Faster stronger than the one before
The candlelight dims as the sunrise overtakes
I sit in awe

Another day before me
Another day for trains
Traveling and passing
Not to be unnoticed

No Matter where you find yourself today,
you are amidst the rhythm.   •
You have the ability to participate and/or observe.
There's no right or wrong choice.
Just an awareness that you're not alone.

Wouldn't surprise me one bit if you find
joy watching others move about.

Riding in a shuttle driven by a man from Cameroon—

He came to the USA to live a better life and loves it here.
I am fascinated by the adventurous souls who
pick up and move to another country.
Sometimes a reminder like this is all we
need to appreciate our surroundings.
Realize your adventure today.
You're living an abundant life!

Thank you for lifting my spirit so I can be the best possible me for those I love and those I have yet to meet.

While on a visit to Spearfish Canyon in South Dakota, I watched a drake swim with several mallards. Next to the pond was a sign quoting Frank Lloyd Wright—"Study nature, love nature, stay close to nature. It will never fail you."

Spearfish Speaks

Canyon walls
Rimmed with unfathomable growth
of tethered aspen and pine

Lift our hearts, our minds
To understand unfinished quests
in traces of rockslides.

Let's steer our thoughts to positivity. Each time you catch yourself having a negative thought, rewrite it in your brain and do it with compassion.

Oh, Happy Heartbeats, you amaze me.

Man, Warrior, Friend

Man, Warrior, Friend
Complex with contradictions.
Feet firmly planted, yet you sway
in a world you didn't ask for.
The heart's conscious begging sounds
hollow thumping on the wood block.
The slow rhythmic beat
gathers ancestors to be with you,
to stimulate awareness of destruction
while loving all that is good.

Nurture yourself by observing
and relishing the ordinary.
Discover the rhythms of your daily life
and the elements that surround you.
If you notice something that makes you smile,
hold onto it for a moment.

Grateful for the Ordinary!

Autumn Light

I took an enchanting walk in the autumn light
pondering the sedum bloom
its color reminding me of the soft sweetness of raspberries
on my lips
bringing anticipation of next year's yield.

The mountain watches
its trees cast shadows like long eyelashes
across the valley floor
to where a rickety fence, like a worn out foe,
teeters, yet still tries to make a stand.

Turning myself into the wind
so that I may breathe even deeper
as if my lungs were in my boots
aware of posture, I straightened.

Tears forged
liberate the bison jaw and bones
that once roamed free
on the very land that once held me.

Recognizing when to repurpose items or to give them to someone else to enjoy is a form of meditation.

We all have things we "Have to Do"
but what happens when we change our approach to
"Today I Get to Do"?

Obligation versus Opportunity

By the way, have you looked outside?
The sunlight is amazing and so are you!

How our bodies work
and the freedom we have to move about
are often taken for granted.
As you move through this day, notice your gifts.

Feeling grateful for movement.

Technology

I've been repeatedly told I'm not technologically savvy. I beg to differ. I worked eight years in medical offices, filing claims and reports and using computers. In fact, in the early 90s, I was an IT tech working for a mail order company in the wee hours, generating reports for the upcoming business day while my husband and children were tucked in bed.

It wasn't until several years later that I discovered my time spent away from the office to raise our children caused me to fall out of the loop. By the time I re-entered the workplace, technology had advanced leaps and bounds.

Childbirth was easier than the frustration I've experienced trying to become proficient on the computer. I'll give my husband and sons credit for their patience. What none of us will ever understand is how I arrive at such situations on the computer. Seriously, my eldest spent two hours on the phone walking me through the steps to resolve an issue. I was under the desk, phone in one hand, trying to sort a basketball-size matrix of cords with the other; back up top to read the messages; back underneath the desk to restart the modem and check the power strip. I was breaking a sweat! This was all before iPhones. It wasn't until we had damn near given up that something I said registered with him. I believe it had something to do with a wireless mouse. In less than a minute he solved my problem! None of what we had just spent the last two hours doing was relevant. Nope. Just a little switch on the mouse. I'll be forever grateful, and we sure had a good laugh. I may have driven him to drink.

Fast forward to 2016. I was alone in Georgia waiting for the movers to come. My husband had already started his new position in Massachusetts. Our kids didn't live nearby. In fact, they weren't even in the same state. I needed to get a few groceries to tide me over for a couple of days before I departed the South. I picked up a few items and went back to my car to discover I had locked the keys in it. I had my phone and thought about calling a locksmith but remembered from a past experience they were pricey. Then it occurred to me, I could redeem myself and make my kids proud and use Uber for the first time. They said it was really affordable and simple to do. I knew I needed to download the Uber app and so I did. I watched my cell phone's remaining battery life rapidly drain as the app twirled about on the screen downloading. I could see my charger locked in the car. I knew just enough about Uber to know that they communicate with you live, and I wondered how long the battery lasts when it's in the red. Finally, my screen opened and Uber wanted to know what color of car I wanted. Really? I couldn't care less. Do you have any idea how hot it gets standing on a paved parking lot in Atlanta? I'd sweated through my clothes, and I just needed a ride to my house to get the spare keys. I drove a black car so I hurriedly picked a black car before my battery died. I didn't pay attention to the rate, as the seconds were flying by.

Within minutes a beautiful black Lincoln Town Car showed up. I couldn't believe it! I thought, no wonder the kids love using Uber. They're riding around in affordable luxury. Who wouldn't use Uber? I was so excited, I wanted to call my kids right away to let them know of my achievement, but I couldn't because the phone battery was exhausted. The driver opened the door and I stepped inside with my flip-flops on and my plastic bag of groceries. In the mile and a half drive to my home, the air conditioning took me from relief to being chilled to the bone in my damp clothes. I asked him to wait so that he could take me back to my car. As you might have already guessed, my house key was also on the key ring locked in my car. I ran to the back of the house and was able to leverage a window open and crawl through to get the spare keys. When we arrived back at the grocery, the kind driver opened my door and thanked me for using Uber's Black Car Service. A locksmith may have been cheaper, but when I shared my experience with my kids, that was priceless!

Hmmm, you swayed a little yesterday—
how about a little saunter today?
And yes, yes, you should hum or sing a little too.
Even if it's only on the way to your house.

Grateful when you shine your light!

Do you know the times when you're in a hurry and you want life to respond exactly as you imagined . . . but it doesn't?
Maybe it's because we're supposed to slow down enough to enjoy the experience.

Grateful for another Sunrise.

Whether you're running a marathon or walking to your car, stop to see where you came from.
Recognize your feeling for that single moment.

Sweet!

Lost Car

A woman approached me in the parking lot of the shopping plaza after dark, asking for my help to find her car.

We walked up and down the aisles of cars unable to locate her '97 red Toyota Forerunner. She exclaimed, "I know I've parked my car here. Someone's stolen my car!"

I asked, "Is it possible you've parked anyplace else other than where you've described?"

"No! Someone has stolen my car!" she said. "You're not going to believe this, but I am a professional organizer."

With those words, I began to wonder if she was playing with a full deck. I have the tendency to attract such individuals. My close friends and family will testify to this phenomenon. In fact, it happens so frequently, they believe I am a "Loony Magnet."

The Ulta store was well lit, so I walked inside and requested they call mall security to help this woman. The clerk suggested her car may have been towed if she mistakenly parked in a handicap spot. I went back outside and asked the distraught, petite, 5'2" woman if this was a possibility. Dumbfounded, she replied, "I don't think so but my important papers are in my car." I called Couriers Towing for her to see if they'd recently towed a red Forerunner.

"No, Ma'am, we haven't."

Security arrived and she recited the entire scenario. Now I could've left, but that's not my nature. I stayed and listened.

Security officer: "Does anyone else have keys?"

Woman: "No, and it takes two keys, one to get in and another to start it."

Security Officer: "Ma'am, a '97—seems against the odds . . . anyone would . . . steal it."

I left her with Security and took another drive to search the plaza. This time, I drove into different sections, and whattaya know, there was her RED FORERUNNER with a bumper sticker, "A man is not a financial plan."

I drove back to let them know I had found her car over in another lot just as Security was reporting the stolen vehicle to the local police. When I told her where it was parked, she responded, "You're absolutely right! I was going to leave the plaza but when I saw traffic was so heavy, I decided to stop and get a cup of tea."

Lunar Challenge

Need you be reminded of the full moon?
Of course, people and things get a little off kilter—
okay, maybe a lot, but you have the knowledge
and skill to navigate this with ease.

Gotta Love Awareness!

Live Your Truth

Accept to live your truth.
Leave wounds behind.
Move forward with confidence.

Acknowledgments

To all who have inspired, encouraged, endured, and believed in me, thank you.

You have stood by me with your support. Many of you have read my words, at least some of them, and recognized a time we've shared is now a relatable poem, story, or thought. I am so grateful to be blessed and rich with family, dear friends, and acquaintances all over the country and beyond.

Special thanks to the people who have helped to improve my writing: Judy Burch, Rich Mills, Sarah Crawford Johnson, Dorothy Leach, Heidi Ruby Miller, Darla Karchella, Bill and Jacqui McMahon, fellow Pennwriters, and members of the Western Writers of America, the Nebraska Writers Guild, and Maryland Writers Association. Julie Haase, my editor, your discerning eye has become invaluable for creating my voice.

Immense gratitude to my husband Tim for enduring my unique desire to evolve. And to my family, without you I would not have developed my perspective or become the woman I am today. Your presence in my life means the world to me.

A couple of signs hang in my office. The one I've had the longest reads "Go Over, Under, Around or Through but . . . Never Give Up." I can attest to living by these words. I've come to realize I can figure most things out when I invest enough time and research. This doesn't mean I will agree with the results or they'll satisfy my quest, but there is a sense of accomplishment from the knowledge I've gained.

Lastly, in the spirit of publishing this book, the second sign reads, "What If I Fall? Oh, but darling what if you fly."

About the Author

Lori Joseph has drawn on her life experiences as an artist, wife, mother, photo stylist and producer, for inspiration in her writing. Always observant, she often writes about our connection to the environment. The Pennwriters awarded Joseph first place in their annual poetry contest with her poem titled "Wasserfall." It was the first poem she'd ever written.

Soon after, Joseph completed "The Homestead Collection," a selection of poetry based on photos of the mountain west taken by photographers Tim O'Hara and Terry Wild. The collection was published online by *Clerestory Poetry Journal: Poems of the Mountain West.* Joseph also framed the images with her poetry to create a touring exhibit that has shown in Massachusetts, Wyoming, and Maryland. Her work has been published by the Union Pacific Railroad, *JustBeU* magazine, and the

Nebraska Writers Guild in their poetry chapbook *How It Looks from Here* and in their anthology *Voices from the Plains*, 2nd ed.

In addition to writing, Joseph offers the A2A workshop, which can be tailored for individuals or group team building. Contact Lori@LoriJoseph.com to schedule a workshop.

17048319R00064